D0997386

To my little friends
Vassilis and Katerina.
A. D.

1st edition April 2018

ORIGINAL TITLE Αγγελική Δαρλάση, *Η Ελιά*,
Μεταίχμιο 2017

TRANSLATED FROM THE GREEK BY Vasiliki Misiou
ILLUSTRATED BY Emilia Konteou

ISBN 978-618-03-1457-1
AUXIL. COMPU. CODE 81457
C.E.P. 4340 C.P. 9750

© 2017 METAICHMIO Publications
and Angeliki Darlasi

Bookstores
1. 18 ASKLIPIOU STR., 106 80 ATHENS
TEL. +30 210 3647433, FAX: +30 211 3003562
Internet Site: www.metaixmio.gr
e-mail: metaixmio@metaixmio.gr

2. POLYCHOROS, 118 IPPOKRATOUS STR., 114 72 ATHENS
TEL. +30 210 3003580, FAX: +30 211 3003581

ISO 9001

Angeliki Darlasi

The
Olive Tree

Illustrated by
Emilia Konteou

Myths and Legends of Modern Greece

Translated by Vasiliki Misiou

METAICHMIO

On mountain slopes and hills,
my child,
a tree grows known around
the world.
By north winds it is untouched
and by the heat remains unharmed.
It's always green – in winter holds its leaves.
Its fruits are juicy, fleshy, and so rich.

It is a symbol of both peace and hope,
it is the famous olive tree that feeds us all.
And from the past to present times
it's been so close to many people's lives.

When fall came and its fruits began to fall,
all people got prepared and waited for
the harvest to begin, the olives to be great
and fill the empty jars at home.

Long, wooden sticks and olive sheets they had in hand,
while heading to the harvest all again.
And while they worked, they sang and laughed
as olives fell onto the sheets under the tree's shade.

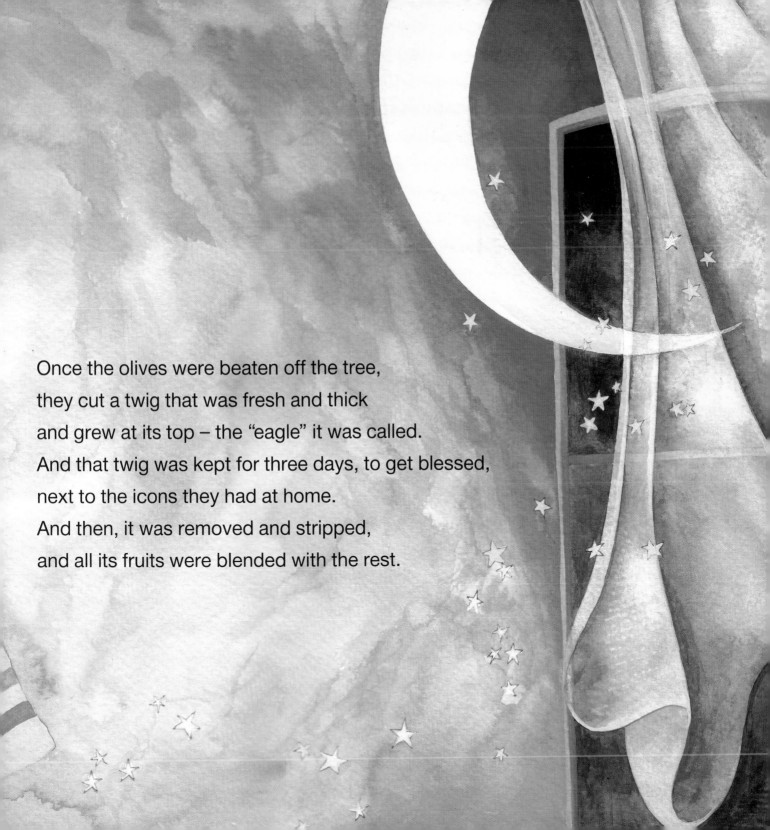

Once the olives were beaten off the tree,
they cut a twig that was fresh and thick
and grew at its top – the "eagle" it was called.
And that twig was kept for three days, to get blessed,
next to the icons they had at home.
And then, it was removed and stripped,
and all its fruits were blended with the rest.

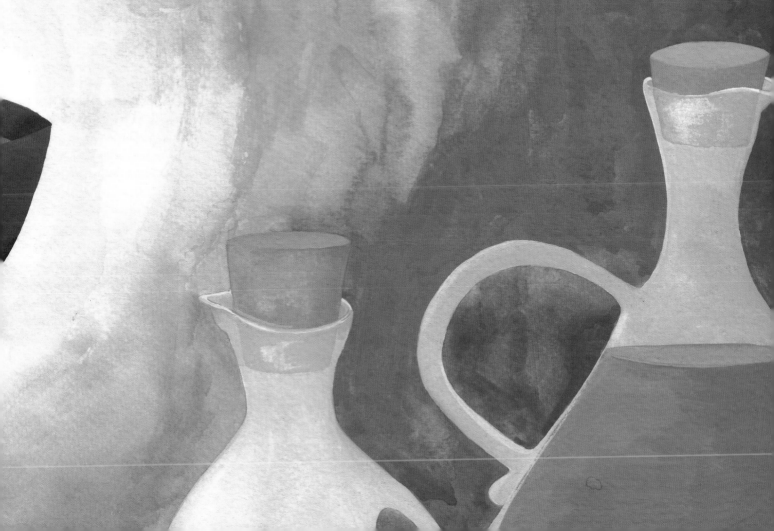

All olives were believed to be blessed this way
and their grace conveyed to the oil made,
which they expected to be rich
to feed the children, the old, the young,
and fill the oil candles that lit consolingly in the dark.

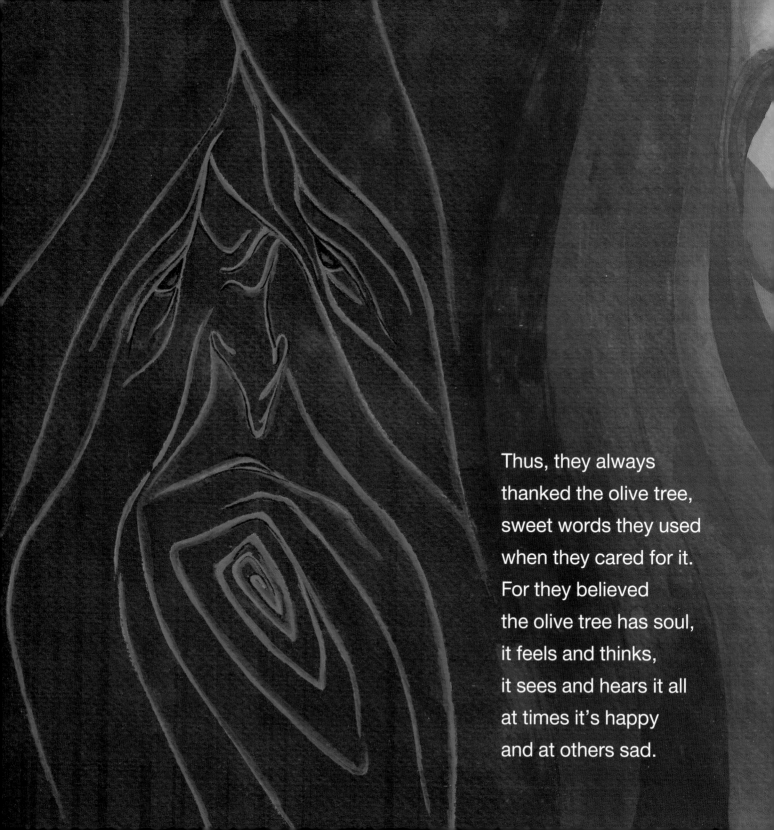

Thus, they always
thanked the olive tree,
sweet words they used
when they cared for it.
For they believed
the olive tree has soul,
it feels and thinks,
it sees and hears it all
at times it's happy
and at others sad.

Whenever they picked olives, thus,
they always left some on the branches
so that the tree didn't feel bad
or think they want to grab
unthankfully all olives, leaving none.

The tree then would stand happy and would grow,
and wish its olives to be sweet and rich
so that all people would enjoy their taste;
for joy is always greater when it's shared.

Alas if they were greedy and forgot
to leave some fruits and rather picked them all.
Embittered then the olive tree would sigh
producing bitter olives, its soul's tears.

At times such was its anger, grief, and pain,
its sorrow for the harshness they displayed
leaving its branches fully barren
that, being deeply hurt, it withered away to its roots.

And those who had been greedy got no fruits
and lived dark days of great famine.

So if you ever find yourself, my dear,
next to an old and knobby olive tree,
sit close to its roots, under its shade sit
and open your kind heart to listen to its stories.

For it has much to say,
advice to give,
so wondrous things from
ancient times to relive.

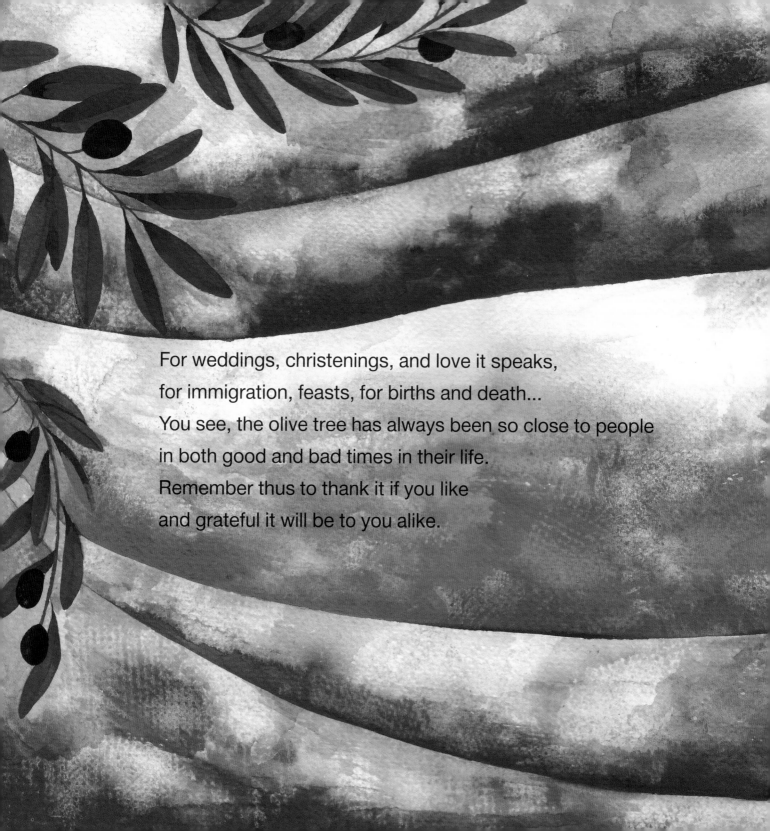

For weddings, christenings, and love it speaks,
for immigration, feasts, for births and death...
You see, the olive tree has always been so close to people
in both good and bad times in their life.
Remember thus to thank it if you like
and grateful it will be to you alike.

If these are true,
I cannot really say.
On older people's
stories I rely.

Just bear in mind, my child,
that words in tales
are sweet to the soul
and sweetly say it all.

ABOUT THE SERIES

This series of legends and stories of Modern Greek tradition emerged from the need to remember again, even for a while, some things that seem to be forgotten – like our grandmothers' old embroideries and white needlework which have been buried in the closet as they don't match modern furniture; but also in an effort to be enchanted again by the words of old times, words that comforted people and kept them company, words that tried to explain whatever scared or charmed them in the past and passed on orally. And since it is about oral tradition, the use of the Greek iambic 15-syllable verse[*] –a verse that is linked to everyday language– offered me a natural, almost self-evident, link between past and present in order to retell the narratives, to share them with our children; now that we don't narrate stories the way people did in the past...

The material used has been mainly retrieved from Nikolaos Politis' collection and publication of folklore material, but also from the stories I remember "the older ones saying". I chose some of those stories which made a strong impression on me as a child and made my mind...travel.

This is hence a series that offers us a reason for reviving the words said by older people.

ANGELIKI DARLASI

. . . .

THE OLIVE TREE

There are many worship traditions, beliefs and customs related to the beloved olive tree all over Greece. The story in this book is based, on the one hand, on Greek oral tradition as it has been recorded in the book of Kostas Romaios *Close to the Roots – A Study on the Mental World of Greek People* (Hestia Bookstore, 1980), and on the other hand on the narratives (and moralizing speech) I heard as a child when I visited my grandmother Angeliki's village.

---

* The rhythmic pattern chosen in the English version is *blank verse* (unrhymed iambic pentameter), although not followed slavishly. *Blank verse* provides a less rigid and at the same time more natural flow. Like the Greek iambic 15-syllable verse, it offers great flexibility, an underlying rhythm and musicality.

Angeliki Darlasi was born in Athens, where she still lives and works. She has a BA in Theatre Studies (University of Athens) and an MA in Performance Studies (Royal Central School of Speech and Drama, London). She has worked in theatre, cinema and television. She is a writer, playwright and tutor for adults and children in creative writing and theatre.

She has collaborated with Metaichmio Publications for her books: *The Fates*, *The Mermaid*, *The Olive Tree* and *The Stone Boat* (Myths and Legends of Modern Greece), *The Awaken Princess* and *The Mermaid Who Went Ashore* (Little Goodnights series), *When the Statues Went Away* (novel), *The Boy in the Loge* (novel).

Other books of hers include: Illustrated books: *Bad Boy* and *The Tree that Had Wings*. Novels: *Dream guardians and the Lighthouse of Dreams*, *My name is... Cloud, or the Unwritten Pages of a Girl Called Nefeli*, *When We Hid an Angel*, *Dream guardians*. And the CD: *Alice in Wonderland* (music theatre adaptation).

She is the recipient of many awards. Her work has earned her a place on the Honour List of the International Board on Books for Young People (IBBY) and on the international list of the 2010 White Ravens (International Youth Library in Munich). She has won an award for the Best Illustrated Book for children and young adults and an award for the Best Novel for young adults both from the Greek section of the IBBY (the Circle of the Greek Children's Book), the Greek National Prize for Children/Youth Literature, the Greek National Prize for Children and Youth Theatre, a commendation in the Play Contest organized by the National Theatre of Northern Greece, and a prize in the Playwriting Contest for New Playwrights (Notos Theatre – General Secretariat for Youth).

For more information: www.facebook.com/DarlasiAngeliki/

Mail: angeldarlasi@gmail.com

· ·

Emilia Konteou was born in 1984 in Irakleio, Attica. The moment she started speaking she wanted to use words to build a world of her own. One day the words grew big and they were not enough. Then she started using shapes. When this was not enough too, she added colours. Looking at the final outcome, she felt there was something missing and she added dreams, a spoon of hope and as much love as possible. Since then she has been illustrating whatever inspires her from children's books to stories with a happy or sad end. She holds a BA in Sketch-Comics-Cartoon (cum laude) from the AKTO educational group and has been awarded the second place in the contest held for new talents by the magazine "9" of *Eleftherotipia* newspaper. She works as an illustrator and has collaborated with many publishing houses.

Angeliki Darlasi
The Stoneboat
Illustrated by
Theda Mimilaki

Myths and Legends of Modern Greece

METAICHMIO

Angeliki Darlasi
The Fates
Illustrated by
Sandra Eleftheriou

Myths and Legends of Modern Greece

METAICHMIO

Angeliki Darlasi
The Mermaid
Illustrated by
Iris Samartzi

Myths and Legends of Modern Greece

METAICHMIO

Angeliki Darlasi
The Olive Tree
Illustrated by
Emilia Konteou

Myths and Legends of Modern Greece

METAICHMIO